earthling

steve healey

COFFEE HOUSE PRESS

Minneapolis

COPYRIGHT © 2004 Steve Healey
COVER ART AND DESIGN © Randall Heath
AUTHOR PHOTOGRAPH © Mark Wojahn
BOOK DESIGN Linda S. Koutsky

Coffee House Press books are available to the trade through our primary distributor, Consortium Book Sales & Distribution, 1045 Westgate Drive, Saint Paul, MN 55114. For personal orders, catalogs, or other information, write to: Coffee House Press, 27 North Fourth Street, Suite 400, Minneapolis, MN 55401.

Coffee House Press is a nonprofit literary publishing house. Support from private foundations, corporate giving programs, government programs, and generous individuals help make the publication of our books possible. We gratefully acknowledge their support in detail in the back of this book.

LIBRARY OF CONGRESS CATALOGING-IN-PUBLICATION DATA

Healey, Steve
Earthling / Steve Healey.
p. cm.
ISBN 1-56689-164-7 (alk. paper)
I. Title.
PS3608.E238E17 2004
811'.6--dc22
2004012790

FIRST EDITION | FIRST PRINTING
1 3 5 7 9 8 6 4 2
Printed in the United States

earthling

contents

four

five

six

one

when you commit a crime

A pinch of salt causes
the boiling to begin,

and a tribe of dice rolls
down the lucky slope.

They come to a rest
near the lucky fire and reveal

the terms of my punishment.
They stand me

waist-deep in the shallow end
of a cool swimming pool.

They call me *drinking straw*
because I appear to be bisected

by a transparent beverage,
an illusion caused by refraction.

My lower body sips
the shallows and asks for grace,

a song takes my upper body
to the deep end.

The kind of song that hates
boats for performing so well

in this slippery square,
grace for stealing my own

distance from the fire.
If you look hard enough

into the sleep of a fish,
say the dice, you will find

the correct method for throwing us.
The total number of black dots

represents the years ago
tomorrow began.

tilt

Long after winding down
the party keeps winding down.

It smiles in the gridlocked smoke
long after swizzle sticks tell the journey
about no one going home with someone
along the underground story lines,

and I remember the part where
you said you can't even remember
the good parts. Here's my self-portrait

as conveyor belt, I've no further
questions. Here's the case of missing bridges

or the justice system of little girls,
I've heard them chant like pickled banshees:

bubblegum, bubblegum, in a dish,
how many pieces do you wish?

One, two million, a deluge of yes,
yet missing from the deluge can be sweet,

a no or two placed carefully at points
of least resistance, so heaven's close enough
to taste. I wonder if that's the voice

who took me across the water last week
"halfway between ice ages."

It was mild, yes, with scattered clouds,
which came to see us as ideal listeners
squinting at the silent parts.

Imagine receiving Aaron Burr's bullet
on the cliffs of Weehawken, and according
to their address, Lucy and Ricky
lived at the bottom of the East River,

says the voice that becomes an ocean
no one knows exactly where.

It's all atoms anyway, largely
excreted by faraway stars as part
of an old bedtime story. This carbon atom,

for example, has never died, and since
we've never been to sleep, how many
bridges have we built to feed
this megalopolis? Only later

do they offer the consolation of not
having been, I mean it's never dark here,

and look at those trees happy to wallow
in ignorance of autumn's coming.

Or the fruit, vibrant gray outside
the bodega. Or the fruit, balanced on
technicolor curves. Or the cut flowers,

like men in a tilting city. Or a man curls
around a fountain while a water blossom

keeps petal-falling back around its
pushing through. Or a man keeps

circling the park, nibbling it
with his yes-shaped mouth.

small winter

This is the white that was everywhere.

This is the sound of it,
the white cake born that last first day
chewed alive by our watery teeth.

This is the frozen lake and the way
we walked over it with ships

for feet, the way fish spoke
to our toes through the ice.

This is the age of ice followed by horses,
followed by engines. This is how
we hatched a bundled flotilla of you,

you, and you, how your winter skin
lagged behind its pigment, at first

wanting to kill the bad engines,
then growing nice and snow-blind.

Dear white, these are your eyes,
this is the crow plucking letters
from your velvet bag eyes.

Eventually an alphabet will talk,
words like *tiny* and *hark*,

eventually a conversation will veer
into the kind of temporary shelter

that skins trees alive and stacks them
as catacomb walls, except this catacomb
is full of white and laughing.

I just wanted to give this to you
and give you to the sound of it.

Whether I'm saying it right
or whether we took something
for the pain or it flew from our hand

into our blood, this is the same story
that ends in amnesia. These
the same trees who saved us
from the horizon by telling us to forget

where the map ends. I don't know
how we ever didn't live in that wood
with the burning hair until now,

and now it bends us (again)
with the bending light,

it makes the porch bloom
with birdhouses and ashtrays.

Dear winter, when you become
our new mistakes, please bring to our lips
something to breathe, bring another cracker

heaped with fish eggs, and if these
become too many lives to sing,
please bring that intoxicated melodica

and we'll play it while you knit
those little people (us)
under one icicled roof.

Or no roof at all, I don't think
it matters. Their huge voices still stand

so silently in the cold and their breath
escapes like a secret pillow
to a distant dream system,

but this isn't there. It's here,
and this does matter. Even now
you may see black wings up close,

you may hear them say, don't be afraid,
let the sky be an example, silently
count the ticks till midnight,

err on the side of grace, zero gravity,
dandelion ghosts, then hurl yourself
onto the vanilla ice-cream Earth.

This is the clearing, this is here
for a few seconds spitting
scintillas into the air,

and these are the stars.

two

my wrist split open

because I flew through the glass door when
the bad animal scared me, but the doctor
said I could go to the beach because
my cut would like to drink salt. Then

I went in the ocean with my happy boat,
a wave swallowed us and my boat swam away
from my hand. A shiny man told it to come back

but it kept going all the way to Spain
and swam into the hand of someone who looks
like me. They have water everywhere,

they have ice cubes and eyes, and sometimes
it rains on TV. When it doesn't rain
the backyard splits open and I hate something
in there that wants to drink me like juice.

When the clock points out the window
we make the bathtub hold its breath and turn
the knobs. I get inside and it doesn't rain
in China till we let the dirty water go.

When the hiccups come I hold my breath
so little men can run around and fix me
while my heart keeps counting *one potato, two.*

If I breathe too soon my hiccups come back
and kill the little men. Then I have to pee,

I'm sitting in the pew and no one can leave
so my legs try to fly. Before bed I try
to pee but it's never enough. Sleep looks
like the inside of a marble, and sometimes

there's a hole in my bed, and something I hate
in there drinks me and pees in the sheets.

Then the marble rolls down the stairs
and I run up the hill and tell the good birds
not to be afraid. They say the phone is for me

and I climb into the box of my teeth
and say the words that run through wires

into faraway ears. The moon is the color
of a pill that tastes like nothing,
and it climbs into the box.

my friends are on fire

Most of what happens to them doesn't take up space
but is a kind of music that can be seen

and absorbs bubbles of silence
in greater or lesser quantity depending on
how sleepy they feel. Now they proliferate

like dandelions, now they are extinct—
is how the chorus might go. I am they
who often survive the invisible civil war

and celebrate by eating an animal
that's been smoked for a full rotation of the Earth.

It's like a hula hoop eating one of my friends whole,
or the inventor of the hula hoop dying to send
his bellybutton into orbit. At this point

they take threads from the sky's four corners
and make a hat I'm instructed to wear
as protection, and everyone boards
the happy tugboat to chug around the city island.

Notice that the wind is there, and moisture
refuses to evaporate quickly enough.

Notice the one loose thread dangling
from above, and how hard it is
not to look directly into the sun
with all that stardust in their veins.

When the dewpoint strains verisimilitude,

and they offer a little spittle to the sun
to help cure the blind, and those
fireworks the night before,

they remember being touched,

they consider defenestration a falling in love
with clouds, yodeling to the grave—

they who sip flames, they sip hot sauce
from bronzed baby shoes, they have
the city coming out of their skin,

they have tall buildings to braid,

bridges to sandwich the newlyweds
who've just spoken the words, and the words go:

I do not want to live in the goo of doubt,

I want to sing to the particles and waves
how much you rock, I want to feel the womb

from which my friends emerged so long ago
to follow a light across the flatlands

to the promise of water and salt.

my debut

Standing in the backyard of my nation
I keep looking at my new shoes.

They're like two small arks
saving my feet from the truth.

Perhaps it is only a pupil-colored bird
deciding how things will look.

The commas coming out of your eyelids,
you can toss them over your shoulder.

Says the cookie's red fortune,
someone will visit you soon.

Water will creep into the backyard
and change the meaning of the arks.

Confession: I'm rehearsing things to say
to you, I'm tired of being scared.

This is why we descend from the mountain,
to be as fruit, blueberries or pears,

and still animal, shackled to my ankles.
Inside my feet, miles and movies of them,

a yellow car driving too slowly sees
angels who never appear to move or sweat,

a page of old snow never slips off a roof.
Chances are, if you stand still long enough,

a holy war is there, like a mountain
or self-medication, your fingers

begin to let go what they only imagined
holding so long. This scene, for instance,

a woman biting a Bartlett pear,
I see her curvaceous indifference

to my new shoes, but take it blindly.
My debut grows so quiet, even with a star

sleeping in my ear, I can hear the light
falling on this smooth smooth ocean.

why we continue

Because nerves need more staircases to climb,
streets need skids to absorb, eyeballs
see only antonyms gathering on horizons,

even a round Earth dreams flatness,
a muscle stretches from here to heaven

like a braille menu of stars, because kids
go down on each other on a basement couch,

a clock is always visible, oxygen diminishes,
small windows promise transportation
and a future of pickled matrimony,

years inhale property tax, attics fill
with bat excrement till homeowners sell it
as fertilizer, and roofs are tightly sealed,

each bat is an object of extermination
while mosquitoes proliferate madly,
piercing virgin skin, stealing blood before
it circulates back as predictable wisdom

to the heart, a parched dowser nears
a suburban mirage, what were once
mountains are neighborhoods made of sand

where those who wake against a body
weigh the opportunity cost for kindness,

fingers grow guilty for begging a dime's worth
of candy, because a signature grows illegible,

and as mercury drops, seconds drip,
an unnameable ailment erodes the bosom,

because a prison song repeats impossible gods,
a greeting card arrives to explain how
a friend suffered an "accidental overdose"

and emerged from a coma having forgotten
the past several years, because there's a place
where conversations and faces go,

where we find the soldiers gazing at us
from the sepia war, because we believe.

the underwater reading

What would have to do with the sea?
—ELENI SIKELIANOS

Afterwards we went each to our own small white desert
and wrote about seahorses. Much reference was made
to the prehensile tail and its balancing effect.

Q saw it trying to grasp the slippery water
while Y noted how it allowed the upright body
to bob like a bone-plated kite. As X put it,

a seahorse traverses its own submarine skies
propelled by a microeconomy of dorsal fins.

Thus we appeared to be recovering an ancient lightness:

one could wake the others by whispering
the word *swim*, and the swimmers abandoned
their hands like spent shadow puppets.

According to O, there's one sunrise and it never stops,
it wears flaming tubercles for anyone to see.

Likewise, a certain store sells nothing
but moments caught forever in amber:

my favorite, added B, is tree resin
found "washed ashore on the Baltic coast"
that functions as a clock. As an after

chooses its noon to follow,
tock after tick, it doesn't forget
to precede evening. And as you'd expect,

the part in the film about *le petit mort*
did precede a well-executed egg deposit into the male,

he being, famously, the giver of birth
who hiccups the tiny translucent babies
from his swollen belly. Still,

our attention was swallowed by something
we never really saw even though the camera
lived underwater. We could've been on dry land,

said A, listening to the leaves *la la la*
between dark and not dark.

We could've unicycled into space.
We had bodies to love.

things we say

in unison, to resemble a cathedral,
to be pretty and healed,

not worthy to receive you,
flesh wafer and blood grape.

You the star of what we say
after swallowing, sucking teeth,

considering how the priest shaves
his face, still hungry, multiplied
by zero, divided by scars,

thin enough to exit and say things
in motion. Like a wheel turning north
from a parking lot under scarlet skies,

driving through air across a bridge
not found on a lipstick map.

Like branching toward an electric vacancy
to hear the silent things we say
bathing, soaking our breasts.

Because we don't die at the same time,

we don't stay here to see this time zone
weep the way a sleeping pill
sees water surrounded by clear glass.

The way water is fireproof,
fire marries what keeps it alive.

The way we say things burning papers,

to a parent dying ungracefully
with cosmetics and old movies,
to avoid being abandoned or infected.

Things we don't mean to neglect
today, the birthday of no one

who recalls the things we said about
what still hurts for the wrong reason,

ex-lovers and ventriloquists
of tomorrow, jazz molecules above lips,

the whole planet curving away
like embryonic light.

i do not know onesies

I do not know English.
—MICHAEL PALMER

I do not know the small person
wearing my quilted outer person.
There is only one, and therefore
I cannot find the baby.

They say the baby is crawling
already, down the street,
but I have forgotten how to crawl.
Therefore, I know that an old person
has just taken a hard fall because
the world has grown fluffier.

It's coming down fierce.
The crows are working hard to keep
the flake drapes sewn to the clouds.
When they say *caw caw caw,*
it means *black needles,*
white thread, swoop.

The baby crawling down the snowy street
is about halfway to the fire station
and will not get there.

Now the crows are eating the snowstorm.
Somewhere between ice and rain.
The fire station is a bookstore.

Like a wheel, the baby develops
a personal relationship with road salt.
Thirst is not an option, hunger
sounds like a deep-fried prayer.

Dear baby, what is it like to be free?
I do not know translation, I'm not
so there, nor do I know how to carry on
this black and white theme.

Here's a Grevy's zebra,
whose true shape is obscured by
its stripes so as to confuse predators.
Here's a prisoner about whom
there's less and less to know.

I need to tell you something.
I cannot find the telephone.
It's somewhere in my hand.

Therefore, I cannot tell you
about the baby crawling down the street,
the door to the bookstore opening,
a cup of warm cider . . .

three

diary of a space suit

I'm not that quiet astronaut they made me out to be,
        but I can barely talk about how difficult the mail is lately.

        At first I think it's just words,
then I feel the mail carrier's fingers
tremble on my elbow and know how much I need them there
        not to fall right off the ground.

When I reach around for those fingers
I find the Northern Plains.

        And here's the question: did I jump or was I pushed?
Was I that quiet astronaut when this whole time
I thought it was you making my blood
move, and who are you,

        would you for even a few seconds listen
to me talk about how difficult the mail is lately?

On Thursday there was an invitation to something,
        I could barely read it, and by Friday,
        to be honest, I missed those words,
I missed their awful approval.

        Where had they gone?
The curtains want to go too,
they want to feel like a butterfly
        flapping through a muggy garden.

        Sometimes I touch that garden,
I miss the crisp February air,
        and for a second I think you haven't been listening
but then your ears still smell like April.

Did I tell you the most difficult part?

        "There are no vehicles of escape:
from now on the topic is intimacy."

Before I was born I was more about not being a body.
        The question: did I jump or was I pushed?

Just to have a roof's story on my face would be enough.
        To see each color spread over its time frame
and surround the castle next door,

it's a perfect Saturday in July, and I don't blame
insects for wanting to freak out the rain.

From this height, tears are more expensive.
        "From now on the topic is intimacy."

In October the squirrel buries my hunger.
        The songbird grows monastic in November,
        leaving December witnessless.

Here astronauts knit the quiet thickly,
        mountains feel so solid they don't exist.

Here's a child's cereal bowl depicting
        the great stars of the universe.

        Good night, they say, drowning.
        Good morning, they say,
swimming through my blood,

        as if it were Sunday,
but there's no mail on Sunday.

how to jump from a moving car

Up ahead a brightness swells where the road bends.
Your finest excretions wait there to be reclaimed.

Misplaced gloves. Bodies who first laid you
on a dendrite carpet, what's-your-face.

Inhale. Fear not the whispery engines,
peel back the dewy dark. Getting there,
said night, makes there disappear.

Driving solves a geometry problem
you left blank long ago, and the blank
produces your view of the parking lot

while cradled in the dental chair receiving
every fluoride treatment of your cavity-prone years.

Back when gasoline smelled like gold milk,
something to douse the frosted flakes
and cocoon-spin with the fumes,

back when news reported only
omissions, turn down the radio.

Tomorrow will harbor the killers
and alchemists, but say the bridge

up ahead wants to retire before
you get there. As self-propelled idea,

the car embodies you. If a storm happens
outside, it syncs with the slo-mo eye.

Call it ghostwriting, whatever,
it knows your name however long
you've lived on this side of the glass.

Let go of shape, your physiognomy
reflected in the tinted corner.

Hail Mary, full of satellites,

let go the planet, suburbs
and dragons, let go buttered bread.

Let go the wheel and listen,
somewhere a stillness takes hold.

henry david thoreau junior high school

You can blend with air.
You can bend around the pond
or math teacher's mouth.
The scar on your arm can whisper
the answer, yes be the answer,
and all the girls named Dawn
(with the Lord still in your good ear).
Like a pine grove, you can hear
fingers be counted, let lunchtime
come forever with its baloney
and noonlight sandwich. But the bell
doesn't ring, it's quiet here
on Earth, and taste, only
the carameled valleys of your molars,
and smell, a house the size
of your smell. Call me lost teeth
and years find a dime in there
to buy an afternoon, I was
bought by a trembling: my eyeball
waterbugs across bright windows,
a janitor pushes moist sawdust
down the hall. Because slowness
gets there, only a matter of when,
and had I given more me
to the homework of my lungs,
maybe just breathing could be
a note to Marvin Alsip. Sorry
you have to sit in the first desk
because of the alphabet, Marvin,
but you can be first to step off
this ark, you can begin
the locker combination song.
The new yearbook is coming out
today, we can say I'm in there,
I'm wearing clothes, that's what
I learned today: pants plus shirt
equals me. That's how to please.
In America, you can please anything

you want to be, you can be a robot
leading a platoon of sticks
around the shoreline, you can be
the shoreline, see the fish flash,
the cannibal clouds. A lightning bolt
may have created the first amino acid,
then what? Then there was a pond
named Walden, and a girl named Dawn,
a stone to skip the silver,
and a skinny ass to rise out
of her gym shorts by the power
of her own hands. You can be
frightened by the signals you receive.
American birds can sound
like millionaires turning up
the volume: they don't care if gravy
kills them, and you can kill me
if you want. The question is
truth or dare, and can you keep
a secret. Can you be a solitary lover,
hoeing beans by the starlight
those branches are willing
to let through.

lungs, nougat, nothing

My last idea appeared
like an archipelago of clouds.

It gathered amphibian flames
and lasted until just now.

Then a tiny storm arrived
without reason or charm,
asking only to be invited inside.

When I came to, the lesson ended.

I learned that membranes
wear many textures, all meant
to hide: lungs, nougat, nothing.

What is fire? A billowy husk.

The more familiar the storm the less
distinguishable from these walls,
the less I lived here. I loved

the smell of a snuffed match,
for example. Where steam went,
I went. A jungle out there
snored like a machine. In here

the jade plant lived for itself,
fanning out soft green earlobes.

It listened to the window bend
as north wind blew, and the room
percolated with ocean sound.

Tiptoe gravity: lifeboat,
wingspan. Song that drank

a cocktail in the dark. No waves,
no particles to speak of.

Curtains, doors. In the next room
a universe beckoned like
a 9000-year-old bird-bone flute,

and the way grew clear:
come here before this avian tune

dawns on you how far from home
waking happens.

You can overhear the hairs
in your ear worshipping a nebula.

If you turn the ocean upside down

it sounds like an animal
bringing its face to the glass.

When the firefighters arrived
the attic was bleeding upward.

The road walked away.

My heels began to murmur:

moonlight, ice.

shirts vs. skins

Worst nightmare: I'm a skin.

I slope over my shoulders,
clavicle, surround my nipples.

Across an abdominal field
to the bellybutton goal:
there a magic shovel digs.

Then I lay me down to
build towers, then a story
about it. I see me afraid

to sweat, made of tiny bricks
wrapped in skin-colored petals
with mustard for mortar.

My shirt's inside me,
we're going to a moon called O.

O is for owls flapping out
from under a technical night.

O is for a sunny sun
and its orchidaceous bee sting

that'll kill my brother
in about five seconds unless
we inject him with special sauce.

Such a mountain may be in the way
of tomorrow if not a wrong turn
in Albuquerque. Suddenly,

Bismarck is the capital
of North Dakota. Then my shirt

comes and makes me addicted
to it, creamy on the inside.

I fall asleep in St. Louis
without me, in the park
of squirrels. They move
too quickly, anyway, darting

from tree to shining tree
like drug dealers checking
their stuff, for stuff can mean

so many things, but you know,
you always know. Life on the side,

a side order of life, extra
salty sweet, because the entrée
is very rare, virtually raw,
the way grown-ups eat it.

Very very, and where went the war?
The party? It takes years for me
to find my shirt, but I do.

We go to a movie together
and hold on tight. We hold
these truths to be self-evident.

as western culture declined
without its knowing

His body is credits rising because
the movie is over. It's a small door open
to the counterfeit light of dead stars

while another vernal equinox, the sequel
to last year's version, comes true,
making day once again equal night.

It's a hand searching for unfamiliar faces
and the syllables they once spoke,

because now he's the only thing
he knows, and there's word this galaxy
is drifting in a different direction

than previously believed. This means
an unknown attracts it, although
it remains intact, iceberg-like,

promoting togetherness, each person
frozen and individually wrapped
inside an enormous shape,

moving simultaneously toward
the same unknown. There's also word

that the Palos Verdes butterfly,
believed to be extinct, has been
"rediscovered" in southern California.

About a hundred of them were found
"flitting around a pocket of deerweed"
next to an oil refinery. This is

visibility after a period of hiding,
proof that the audience had not been
there. Now after three million years

someone has found a near-human skull
in an Ethiopian riverbed, and it had
been there all along. After all that time

it's raining on his shoulders, he hears
it falling from three-dimensional clouds,

clouds his lidless eyes will become one day,
freshly dead in his favorite armchair.

Yes, the sky is broke, the sperm count
on the decline, a funeral procession
an endless corridor of vehicles,

headlights carving the right-of-way,
corpse made-up, well-dressed. And yes,

somewhere in this transparent moment
a mouth reveals an aerial view
of the subdivision he grew up in.

A public clock slips forward
so he'll appear to lose an hour
of sleep. A darkness hugs the globe.

So his value depends not on what
he was but how he's remembered,
wrapped in seamless skin.

He's entering a new wilderness.

It's a garden of enormous fruit
against a skyscraper backdrop.

It's the outer space he's been looking for.

where spring is

I could be a hole
if the room's not already full of them.

We all have insides to let go,
and the room's outside. It's dusk.
I slouch and disappear reading
instructions. White snow all around.

What happens to dusk when you stare
at it? "A fully conscious state,"

this is the song about the space
between branches, "in which normal pain
is not felt." Objects appear smaller

when I miss you, I could swallow
analgesics on a slow rocket,

I could write postcards from the garden:
"It's a Latin garden: *ranuculus,*
prunus, ixia, iris." Then English

flowers nicely after the Black Death;
the fourth wall is rarely missed.

Thank God these few mistakes
have friends, i.e., pilgrims.

A nation can depend on conditioned air,
and surely it's spring there
not just in name. With all the melting,

streets river. Time again to honor
my favorite avant-garde milliner
who wore an exceedingly normal hat

when, just before spring, she
killed herself by the river.

Just before, I mean, some things
haven't happened before. The animals
coming back to life, for example,

they stagger around the house.

four

where shame comes from

The candles are forgetting how
to light the holes in our bodies.
Still, they dine on thunder and hearts,
for soon they will do a quiet crime.

To light the holes in our bodies
satellites steal the script and burn it,
for soon they will do a quiet crime
and save that talk for morning's first blush.

Satellites steal the script and burn it,
the way my clematis has to strangle something
and save that talk for morning's first blush
to pay so much purple interest to the sky.

The way my clematis has to strangle something
when the house is happily numb, hoping not
to pay so much purple interest to the sky.
Only the evidence points to your innocence

when the house is happily numb, hoping not
all your alibis will feel like paper cuts.
Only the evidence points to your innocence,
and in the spirit of full disclosure, I must tell you

all your alibis will feel like paper cuts.
Half the fun is not knowing where that ocean came from,
and in the spirit of full disclosure, I must tell you
if you take the beach away, my ribs will follow.

Half the fun is not knowing where that ocean came from,
like the apostle who came in from the rain,
if you take the beach away, my ribs will follow.
To be in love with my golden mouth,

like the apostle who came in from the rain,
the candles are forgetting how
to be in love with my golden mouth.
Still, they dine on thunder and hearts.

standing in line at the post office

The new stamps had arrived: Houdinis, Warhols, teddy bears.

I was standing in love with a tongue.

Things to do: send rectangles, evasions.
Things that ask no questions, things that happen in the mouth.

The line was more of an arc with lunar ambitions.
"Please bear in mind your earthly vocation."

My bones remembered to stand, to have stood a long time,
not quite a plumb-line from brain to perineum.

Yours truly, they said,
listen: the birth of dancing.

I was launching a bloodless coup against my feet.
I had no mother, no ankles, only
time to live forever in that line.

Do you remember when it seemed the rain
would never stop? Like a new brand of stillness.

What the thornbush felt when
I touched it: roundness of Earth.

Then bear in mind the sound of someone
pounding on the door, wrapped in the sound of showers.

Like Japanese lilacs, you fill my house but don't come in.

A backwards escape artist, the way clothes
wear us, it takes detergent to wash us out.

Like Russian sage, you come in,
but the house is empty and parched.

A just-hatched sea turtle, I know only one thing:
get into the water before dying an early ugly death.

That death, I was standing in line when
I thought about putting it in this missive.

There'd been no movement for a very long time.

The new stamps were learning how to be loved.

I could've used a mountain—
I mean, the softest mirror, I was reaching for it.

Listen: the softest tidal wave.

The subject: coming and going.
"As poll numbers come in, rain rain goes away."

I was standing in what people
are saying about me lately.

the story of pores

In the humidity
we're one inside the other,

knees feel like elbows,
the guesses are all good—

who gets on top, who gets to be
the slope, who gets burned

at the stake gets sprinkled
on the sundae, we don't know.

The story takes less action
when it's about meeting another

moist curve along noon's spiral
into our prehistoric frame,

and elsewhere in the body
a hole grows a shade less smart,

then it's less about you and me
than dusting for fingerprints.

It's dangerous to laugh
as afternoon defogs the water glass

and the hole sees a faraway feather
watching its meat surrender

to the ferns. It's dangerous
and necessary to laugh

at this liquid method of being
inside the other without proof.

The story of pores is about stars
who lead us on a long journey

from bed to another sleep
in the form of tall grass.

interview with a piece of smoke

I can live if all the glass in this neighborhood
sleeps with me or lets me sleepwalk
through the don't-walk paradigm.

Red quickens here and eats the white lines
or throws me from window to window.

My fingers unmarry their prints
and listen, the poly-cotton whispers
pass on Avenue A. On the curb,

tired crutches not going anywhere
once had the urge to fit in the frame,

and because the air is a little medieval today,
flecked with silver codes, it can
bend and bend like cellophane

to include that far castle
with the human but cloud-size head
peering out to give the effect

of nearness. In fact,
everything rests on the tip of a unicorn's horn.

It casts a mile-long shadow: listen,
the tender thunder. It's almost too quiet,

that fear of being damaged, it's like
you telling me how a blister feels

surrounded by maybe 15,000 nerve ends
asking to be rubbed. It's like I'm fluid
slipping away, I'm an Earthling

and a mint farmer saying good-bye
to my rain-soaked rows, I don't know

how anyone keeps breathing while addicted
to that sudden harvest, but it makes me

want to be born again with a caul
over my face. I could be premonition city
with a boy loping through my streets

or a boy going down on the man he'll become—
either way, it's motility the windows want,

and the faster you say it, the faster
I buff my boots with a horsehair brush,
the sooner a horse comes and takes me away,

a white horse with you on it and a horn
jutting from its forehead, the sooner
we come to a piece of music and see

that last night is there wearing
black lipstick, or the lipstick

wears your lips, and we are alive.

circles

Funny how the cookie just sits there
containing its wisdom and raisins.

Or does it secretly expand beyond
the baker's mind to include
the concentric cooing of mourning doves?

Yes or no, the sound is delicious
and recedes before a human ear can have it.

If we reach out things mourn us,
things fly away. Night forgets to light up

and day's excrement knows where
you've been. By the time I get to X,

summer has burned holes in my blank,
the smell proves I'm less figment
than flesh of wayward fruit.

You are here and can go anywhere,
says the talking streetmap.

Under the ocean? Hell, I'd like to be
your alibi for a season, or a circle
meeting you at every point along the curve.

Even July's purple-propellered phlox
feels inert sometimes, then the door
to the closeted garden opens.

A sweetness prevails.

Something lands in the birdbath.

best bond ever

Everyone says Sean Connery
because he has those sleepy eyes

that say even God can't remember
all these secrets. Imagine trying to love
equally every grass blade on Earth,

then lying on the best lawn ever
to feel more like God. While sleeping

I let the green fingers grow through me,
then try to salvage a full-length dream:

waking is where all the best roads
meet the water on my face, and lying there
feels so new it's not possible to talk.

Later, okay, I'll confess aloud:
my father was a covert agent,
and he would've had sex with Sean Connery

any day of the week. Even if they never did it
and this confession goes wrong,
a song may still emerge from it.

A voice is a very naked thing, and even
the best country music is wobbly enough
to say I've had some intercourse,

I've seen some weather, I can't see
where I'm going. Yesterday, for example,

it's summery, kind of nineteenth century:
modern grammar wants to be born,
it wants to exit my mouth.

My best face is where sunny fingers
frequently probe for signs of pain,

and last night I watch lightning
from the broken porch. It's raining
minus signs, my genes mumble
to their briny, obsolete messiah.

Which of my faces gazes
at that flashy necropolis

I don't know, nor am I certain where
Shelley is now, or Descartes for that matter,

but I think about how far away you are
to have an ocean at your feet,

and what you said about the dog
washing up on the beach,
reminding everyone of something.

I'll speak for myself:
the hardest part is receiving the loss

and being very quiet for a while,
touching a certain hole, and believing

these words do more than just lie
on a lot of processed wood bound by
what? The desire to kiss a spy?

My face is the place where
my boat and the water are one,
embarrassment cradles me to sleep,

and yes, my father is the best-kept secret,
he is actually dead.

five

written on papyrus on the island of manhattan

The bony texture lets
a little mystery through,

the upper edge frays into cloud,
refusing to hold my lip.

Then it can begin without answers.

See: a) the air thicken with questions
b) raised hands peel away from a shrug
c) wings multiply from sleeves.

Suddenly a man made of pigeons
steps so delicately around
the idea of flight

that nothing flies away
and the plump equations stay unsolved.

This other variable,
let it stand for the moonflower
from which you sipped rainwater.

Then a white bowl tilts across miles,
a freak system stagnates over time zones.

Is this not correspondence after all?

Better to let the letter
choose its shape or none
of the above. Just walk away

and rain begins to fall.
Violence festoons the avenues,

it's time for the sun to spray umbrellas,
there's a war going on.

Then shades fall away
from their half-lit familiars:

fragile bodies, you called them,
falling apart at dusk. And what is dusk

but something that crawls slowly
up the spine, fleshing
empty space, dissolving differences,

one leg no longer shorter than the other,
both eyelids telling the same alibi.

So thank you for staying awake
or alive a bit longer,

that's a fetching mask,
that's a sweet couple of nebulas
peering through slits in that pillowy sky
you have for a face,

that's a beautiful vein
coursing through your life.

I think the later it gets
the more you remind me of a season
I once knew, or a leaf

considers letting go for the first time
this year, and another leaf says,
wait for me, I'll be your dream thing,

it's getting soporific out here,
it's getting dark,

these colors have called
a cease-fire, although they say

we won't make peace with the pigeons
until they listen to our song,

and first we must practice
for our whole lives.

x-ray blue

Something in my body is broken.

When I look a certain way,
      the house tilts, colors run together.

Fog insinuates the power grid.

      Certain tones of voice do irreparable damage.

You can't take anything back.

Childhood may return as a paper cut.

A new moon lends luminosity to constellations
      (house-like Cepheus, for example).

Just beyond the windowpane,
                tap, tap.

A stone may crack the air where my palm was,
      and this is only a partial account.

I wake up telemetry,

           I take up Butoh dancing,
something else is happening.

I step over the catacombs,

        and something else, twice born,
played back, happens.

Word comes from the island
      that I walk around it,

the middle of the island is burning.

Flames lick a charred swath,
                                  my sacrum flickers.

The deer are inscrutable

except for the antlers they dropped
                          on the ground, what the mice

haven't already gnawed away.

bless you

I say this as the continents continue to drift,
driven by an obscure heat inside the Earth.

I've not been to Antarctica but can tell you
it's the most misunderstood continent,

an apparent imperfection on the globe,
like the bellybutton on a navel orange.

All navel oranges come from one mutant tree
that was grafted with other trees and so on.

This is the difficult life of a seedless fruit,
rescued from oblivion and perpetuated
not by itself but human hunger.

Empires are meant to expand,
blank calendars absorb the stream
of appointments, but who, if not you
or me, can digest that spongy climate,

and when dusk officially exists,
when each thing becomes a fraction of itself,
who can make up the difference?

Tonight a book of names arranges us
in alphabetical order. Everyone is a genius.

Then the sun rises and curiosity wanes,
wanting to be mutual but not always balanced
at the right angle to the ground.

By noon I've completed my trajectory,
returned to my crowded half-acre
to feel the fatigue of Presidents.

My ears fill with pressure,
my heart with little wings.

I slap a mosquito already injecting
my arm, welling for blood.

The authorities will be here soon
to shred my secret documents.

I hear a sneeze, then another.
It's my neighbor on her front porch.

Bless you, I say, although she can't hear me.

melt off

I make the rivers rise—

they want to touch me,
they want to spill outside the lines.

Then isn't it okay if we die sometimes?

Or think of very far rooftops
of sunbaked tiles molded from a woman's thigh,
naturally fluted, repeated music—

O goes my diastole,
                    O favorite superhero.
Her thigh is rivers,
her patience, lock and dam,

foam, cirrus, neurons, bridge
puckered for its first hundred-year sip.

Lub-dub.
          Good morning, electric lines.
Avril, c'est a dire.
                Mercy,
for those who are dying;
for those who wake with a nosebleed,
there is time.
                There are ducks in strange places,
there are girls lighting a door on fire.
Tiny red sky,   tiny red.

Dot, dot,   duck, duck,

soon in fact the crest comes.

Later it's okay to cry. Here a river
          slowly swallowing the necks of trees,

we tell soft lies, we have no quibble
with unbroken buds. Proto-leaves
gripped in tiny green fists.

Top five greatest explorers,
games played swimming in a previous life.
Marco   Polo.

I'll be the blind one:
                    sandbag   brain.

But no river has broken its dike,
                    and a river has broken its dike.

i live two doors down from the powerball winner

She's bathrobed in her backyard,
　　her first cigarette of the day.

The sun just scalped her lilac hedge,
　　she's headlined in orbit.

Doing last night's dishes I soap
　　her queendom logarithmically.

Rooftops free from gravy stain,
　　hills of misc. sink below skyline.

It's all you minus the germs:
　　everyone wins a staring contest.

Everyone either spoon, fork, or knife,
　　that's what I try to remember.

Give the dog a bone for love,
　　find something else to hold.

Those buttercups weren't lying
　　to our chins (weren't the TV people

more beautiful in person?).
　　Same with grass blades, just mown,

greener than green, despite no rain.
　　Not real rain whose rust licks

a few generations, not lightning
　　as your now-disposable time/income.

Dear Director of Human Resources,
　　my *nom de guerre* is good neighbor.

I'd like to be swaddled in the Battle
    of Hastings, as seen on tapestry.

This is only a test. One if by land,
    two if by three. So much quiet,

gossip makes it a garment
    we share like a short alley.

Surround my arousal, if you would,
    with pocket-size Presidents.

According to Pentagon sources
    the bellybutton can't be located,

there's no source. As a result,
    congratulations, and welcome

to the Fertile Crescent. Do you
    need a light? How about some sugar?

dear letter of the alphabet

Much of our history is walking and saying

I don't know, let's spell out a mystery light
all the way there. Let's get bibulous
and do it, I'd like to suck your big toe.

If it smells like lavender, even better.
Like where we've ever walked,

to see if the confluence of two rivers
still murmured, if the blue child
hit by a red car still lived.

Look, my legs are happening,
my steps ask a loaf of house
whose answer is like a butter knife

we've never seen, lit by the moon
in the kitchen as we walk past—

never will see, although the same moon
is lit by your lips all night, maybe

your body has been up without you:
a supposed person clicks on a lamp—

where did the sky go? Maybe it's the way you go
with crows to the hospital and back,
can we ever not return to the body?

It makes me want to stand before your doorknob
again, not even lost or thirsty, not solid

as milk, not snow, not fingernails,
not the answer to how the doorknob works

or how we'll walk through this parched
and gelid season so much fresh dust
held by static electricity.

Like the supposed persons in those drawings
you sent me last summer, they looked
so glassy then but have not broken,
much less disappeared.

Is this the secret they're telling us?

And the animalcules all around,
how do we trust them?

But we do, and we do.

airport bowl

Ten blind pins receive his ball.

Sweat darkening the back of his shirt
takes the shape of Missouri.

Naturally planes roar, he rolls down
the shimmery lane and takes off:

the sound of meat coming back to life.

As if summer weren't light enough,
now there's even more traffic in the sky.

Sometimes he wishes this were a game,
opening his mouth to receive the mountains,
because air says it better up there,

pledging allegiance to the cramps
of several ibuprofen, where nothing occurs,

and Lamb of God, you take away the sins
of the world. Sins I used to imagine

the size of a state, cut from a map
and carried away on that Lamb's back.

It may be a lie how this traveler
takes a few breaths to absorb each angle,
180 degrees, and that pretty hypotenuse.

I also lied about birds being scared
of the ground; it's my palm they fear,

although each is my best friend,
and I love their flying song: please
note the nearest exit and reckon

with your blank, those who never came
close to the Presidential Fitness Award,

those who didn't learn how to kiss
over by the trees. That day you shoplifted
a pebble from the park, then walked
the sparkly streets a supporting character.

We'll call him Mr. Hominid: he barely
survived the great droughts of the Pliocene,

and globalization now coincides
with his bright new music. His temples rain
on parking lots and fields. Again he bowls

an ebony hive toward ten pale people,
and to the Republic, where flesh is idea,
where the flight attendant flows,

wing worships wake, just off center,
just off course, where sunset feeds on yes,

for which it stands, where wrist knows
thumb, inside and out, one nation,

under God, indivisible, with liquid
and lucky socks for all. Go there,

Earthling, alias Tail Wind,
General Washington. Go there,

eyeball, to the end of no.

happiness

is my prickly head.

Is the dusky slope where
quail come to shoot the shit

while their sentinels (from the Latin,
sentire, to feel) feel for the evil bitch cat,

though she's now clawless, i.e.,
feckless as a bird killer.

Happiness is how the baby
fits in my mouth, how
my oldest living blank wants

only to drop herself away from Earth
but no longer thinks like a verb.

July, do you want your last piece of pie?
August, may I be excused?

Whispers a bright document
magneted to the fridge: do not resuscitate.

Still she hates "Quaking Aspen,"
the wall color still off-gassing
after how many years, and the music box

playing "Edelweiss" to make her body
hate the room even more.

How much is enough morphine?

To these windows, she's bite-size,
and beyond, double exposed.

The river's still programmed to shudder
when the wind cracks out of the gorge.

Down below, a delicious golfer squints
through the fading green *longueur*.

The news is red all over.

i'm feeling kind of bifurcated

So it goes, the tale of the changeling
who takes the place of children and oceans,

which is why we can't see the ocean from here
and still lament at dramatic parties

how hard to find hardshell crabs
on this landlocked prairie,

or how long ago we felt the ease
of mutually assured destruction.

Laughter makes softer missiles,
the sky implies. The trick is to forget how.

Magic is what most frightens the magician:
no one recognizes the fruit become fruit,

the pictures rearrange themselves.
To wit: old woman with burning head,

she takes the place of boy holding blue balloon,
who takes the place of dog with dagger

in its mouth. The walls find a new harmony;
what remains is the hunger question,

quite possibly our favorite. We settle
for irradiated beef and mentally follow

its journey. Going, going through
the descending colon of the world.

I call it my friend's house: a carnivorous light
lights on his lips. At night he drools a lake,

buoyed by a pillow, then wakes to drink
water fortified with electrolytes.

This pleases his electric field,
which surrounds him like a bathysphere.

It's winter anyway, come on in.
Does this body have more than one anus?

Once I was tickled to death as a child,
then replaced by a changeling

who took my name and likeness.
Having learned to imitate morning,

all morning he negates stars and wakes
to the ice storm that didn't come as promised.

In turn I grieve the loss of being useless
for a day in a cool smooth country.

Barely a degree too warm, that's all
it takes, and things are infinitely

less lickable. Brought to you
by the very air we breathe—

the saga of my chapped extremities—
and I have to walk to the sun to tell it.

six

asshole of the immanent

I invited all the worms to my place,
        then I wasn't there.

This way I often avoided death.
I'd close my eyes and go, "listen
        to the rain, Harry Truman,"

because the rain sounded
inside his name: my private,
        worm-friendly democracy,

pitter-patter on the furniture.

        Forgive me while I get lost
in this drippy garden so long ago,
it's weeping Japanese eggplants,

it's guitar strums on the moon,
        "gonna drink me a flower
called *la lune,* gonna smell the way home."

I wanted to trust that sound,
whatever sound I made, and the air
replied, "that's a lot of meat."

In truth, it was good eating weather;
        even better, an order of occurrence.

1) My brainchild went to the market.
2) My pony performed a trick,
        then waited all night for the dew.
3) A dewdrop narrated another way
        home: "Dig if you will . . ."

        a single glistening choice
tugs at a grass blade's tip.

It's a Pacific to fly over,
      big enough to forgive

the Rita Hayworth glossy
taped to Fat Man as he free falls
toward that very real city.

      These days they call it
asymmetrical warfare—
that's when one side is losing.

On either side of the perforation,
      it's you times two.

Rogue nation or blue chip,
      a sun called *le soleil*
is available for your consumption.

If you're an airport bar,
no matter, it's good to eavesdrop

on the layovered strangers lubed
on Bloody Marys debating whether
      tornadoes possess an eye.

And as far as that window seems,
our propinquity faded
with the onset of evening
unless we'd lit our separate fires.

Often to make something happen
      I ignored the rain.

Planets filled the system,
and I was about to speak.

      "Thank you for being
such good worms," but I smelled
a terrible peace coming.

the sunny day

This can't go on. If I'm born too late,
with only a thorn for comfort,

or a white lash of moon failing
to hide from the sun, let it be here.

Behind the tinted air, one size fits all.

Sleepers wear an irrational bravery,
they wear architecture, they wake
undreaming loosely-bricked stories,

squinting through a fan of branches
at the scaffolding's puzzle.

And where are the hard-hatted fairies?

Not even the sky's azure contusion
after a storm-licked night knows how

it got there, and I've waited all morning
to be lowered from the unsaid heights.

Maybe a subterranean gossip will find my ears
as I learn to assimilate the bulldozer
tiptoeing through this park, maybe

I'm afraid of the silent grass and instead
of listening to the silence I think

the individual ant behaves irrationally
and in perfect synchronicity with the colony.

I think if each one carried a flake
of my dried blood across the water to Italy,

I could be there in a day if the sun
were not here peeling me like a grape.

the end of soon

Only days left in summer's flux emporium.

Then back to the red-blooded clockwork.
        Meat and ticking ribcage.

The beets are still in the ground.
Tick, tick.
        I have a peeling dream
in which the skin of a cooked thing

slips off to reveal a sliceable heart,
but the ground is cool under
        the green radar of intention:

bird's-eye view of a graveyard for bells.

Consider: a pantomime equals
the space it unfolds, but the beets
        don't know how to move

and we can't seem to change that.

An afternoon moon bobs like a foolscap
on a canopy of purring birds.

Across the street a trellis surrenders
to ravenous morning glories, and you

can hear the skinny whine of a violin
practicing scales, horsehair bow
        rubbing airy tensions away.

There are wild boys puckering
in the alley like translucent ponies

or ships softly colliding in the straits
between seasons.
        Somewhere monks

make a sand mandala, then leave
to let it blow away.
                    Roots hum.

A cloud vivisects a house
and the house fails to wake up.

Just like that, something outlasts us,
light loses belief in our latitude.

Soon we'll wear the new holes of wool.

how to lose a war

I have lost my scarf,
but there is a scarfy feeling.
There is a place I do not hesitate to be born,
not a place but a neck exposed
to the whole crisp world.

Where is my scarf?
Where did you have it last?
If I knew that I would be lost.

The last one standing in a line of one,
I would sit in my own private waiting room.
To sit while standing, that would be
like taking one last hand against
a walk down the street.

Consequently, we are going to war,
there is clearly a material breach.
But first go back, back inside,
the scarf is completely inside my neck,
signified by a scar.

The redness of the scarf remains
in the scar. So perfectly not
here, the scarf is a genius.

It is the doorway through which the naked neck
must pass, it is a street
called Lake unrolling to Lake X,
which lies frozen in the gaze of Lake Y.
The scarf tightens around its own disappearance,
and dusk dashes around the perimeter
like an arson starting fires.

The reason my scarf left me . . .

This is how to squeeze diamonds
from your eyes if you are a soldier going

into reason, but if you are a skater
you must stay on a lake
and listen to the ice.

In fact, sharpened blades make
the best scars on X and Y
when it is exceedingly cold
and worth remembering like childbirth,
although such calculated forgetting
is not lost on the fish.

The scarf is an animal who rejects me,
the reason being the most difficult part
to hear, to have joined the unnameable circus
and returned as gliding action
on the perfect ice.

For the skater in me,
prior to the idea of the scarf
is a feeling difficult to feel.
In a flash of sequined air
it is a feeling on the farthest side of a lake
of a pair of shoulders supporting
a birthday cake.

There is not much time
before a premature eclipse
swallows the sun and the skater's skull
dims in honor of all that did not
get done today or last year.

Consequently, a quick chill comes
across as a loss of scarf,
and the red shadows fly back
through the elongated stoplights of Lake Street.

It is perhaps the longest perhaps
in the whole crisp world,
and what the skater finally wants to feel,
not the final feeling, but the blood
flowing through the neck.

circumstantial

They found a body by the river.

They found the left hand clutching a lodestar.
In the breast pocket, a torn matchbook cover,
black ballpoint map going south.

A song winding through the rib cage
taking hair and skin samples
to naked agoras. They found the face

a palimpsest of looks, darker wards,
moonstruck houses. Something sharp and soft,

a turning corner that didn't say good-bye,
there's a reason for being gone.

We've come far not to end,
and I will always love that
autumns ago even weather seemed slow
to change. We smelled the color between

and found the sun there
a bruise coming the long way home
like the brainchild or last disciple
of a lost summer. We superimposed

dusk over noon and felt a telepathic fish
travel down the neck exerting
pressure against the coccyx.

We were not alone in that aboriginal city,
not far from the river and its barge

called Onward, whose wake was white enough
to remember shores of red, orange, yellow,

shed from the body they found between
the lines, trees unastonished
on the bluff, leaning.

ACKNOWLEDGMENTS

American Poetry Review: My Friends Are on Fire;
Where Shame Comes From

American Letters & Commentary: Where Spring Is

Colorado Review: Small Winter

Crowd: Interview with a Piece of Smoke

Cutbank: As Western Culture Declined Without Its Knowing

Fence: My Wrist Split Open

Interim: Shirts vs. Skins;
Written on Papyrus on the Island of Manhattan

jubilat: Circumstantial

Lit: The End of Soon

nowCulture: My Debut; The Sunny Day

Open City: Tilt; Asshole of the Immanent

Prairie Schooner: Bless You; Things We Say

Swerve: Why We Continue

Verse: Circles; I'm Feeling Kind of Bifurcated

A number of these poems also appeared in the *Fuori* anthologies.

"Interview with a Piece of Smoke" appears in *Isn't It Romantic: 100 Love Poems by Younger American Poets* (Verse Press).

Earthling was written while listening to:
Aerial M/Papa M, Boxhead Ensemble, Gavin Bryars,
Chicago Underground (Duo, Trio, Quartet), The Dead C,
Eric Dolphy, John Fahey, Gastr Del Sol, The Glands,
Godspeed You Black Emperor!, Andrew Hill, Labradford,
Mike Ladd, Language Removal Services, Low, Mogwai,
Tara Jane O Neil, Pan American, Rachel's, Steve Reich,
Smog, Sun Ra, Supreme Dicks, Wingtip Sloat.

This book is dedicated to my friends and family,
with gratitude for all their support.

COFFEE HOUSE PRESS FUNDERS

Coffee House Press is an independent nonprofit literary publisher. Our books are made possible through the generous support of grants and gifts from many foundations, corporate giving programs, individuals, and through state and federal support. This project received major funding from the Jerome Foundation. Coffee House Press also received support from the Minnesota State Arts Board, through an appropriation by the Minnesota State Legislature and from the National Endowment for the Arts, a federal agency; and from grants from the Elmer and Eleanor Andersen Foundation; the Buuck Family Foundation; the Bush Foundation; the Butler Family Foundation; the Grotto Foundation; the Lerner Family Foundation; the McKnight Foundation; the Outagamie Foundation; the Pacific Foundation; the John and Beverly Rollwagen Foundation; the law firm of Schwegman, Lundberg, Woessner & Kluth, P.A.; St. Paul Companies; Target, Marshall Field's, and Mervyn's with support from the Target Foundation; James R. Thorpe Foundation; West Group; the Woessner Freeman Foundation; and many individual donors.

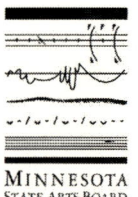

This activity is made possible in part by a grant from the Minnesota State Arts Board, through an appropriation by the Minnesota State Legislature and a grant from the National Endowment for the Arts.

MINNESOTA STATE ARTS BOARD

NATIONAL ENDOWMENT FOR THE ARTS

To you and our many readers across the country, we send our thanks for your continuing support.

Good books are brewing at coffeehousepress.org